SIN

A Christian View for Today

Xavier Thévenot

LIGUORI
PUBLICATIONS

One Liguori Drive
Liguori, Missouri 63057
(314) 464-2500

Imprimi Potest:
John F. Dowd, C.SS.R.
Provincial, St. Louis Province
Redemptorist Fathers

Imprimatur:
+ Edward J. O'Donnell
Vicar General, Archdiocese of St. Louis

ISBN 0-89243-218-7
Library of Congress Catalog Card Number: 84-80872

Scripture texts used in this work are taken from the REVISED STANDARD VERSION / CATHOLIC EDITION of the Bible, copyrighted 1946, 1952 © 1971, 1973. Used by permission of copyright owners.

Excerpts from DECLARATION ON CERTAIN QUESTIONS CONCERNING SEXUAL ETHICS, published by the Sacred Congregation for the Doctrine of the Faith, copyright 1975, and distributed by the Publications Office, United States Catholic Conference, have been used by permission.

Excerpts from the English translation of THE ROMAN MISSAL © 1973, International Committee on English in the Liturgy, Inc. have been used by permission. All rights reserved.

This book is a translation of *Les Péchés: Que peut-on en dire?*, published by Editions Salvator, Mulhouse, France. This English-language translation was edited by Roger Marchand.

Contents

PART ONE

FACTORS
THAT INFLUENCE
OUR SENSE OF SIN

It has become rather commonplace these days to say that Christians experience uneasiness over the notion of sin. For example, people say things like the following: "Sin? I don't even know what it is anymore! To be honest, I have to admit I'm a sinner. But to come up with an actual list of my sins, I don't think I can do it."

In Part One of this book, I would like to reflect on some of the reasons people experience unease when the topic is brought up or when they try to deal with sinfulness in their own lives. To put the problem in focus, let me begin with a few remarks about reflecting on sin and about the importance of such reflection for Christians.

CHAPTER 1

Sin — A Serious Topic for Christians

Reflecting on Sin Raises Personal Questions

No one who reflects on sin is indifferent to it. Advertisements point up this fact. Companies make up ads like "Drink Mixwell Coffee — It Tastes So Good It's Sinful!"

What is there about sin that moves people to buy products?

Sin is good advertising because it takes us back to early childhood experiences. It also ties in with our adult life. For example, try the following experiment with your parish CCD teachers or your parish council. Tell them, "We're going to do a rapid word-association exercise using the word *sin*." Usually, the first reaction you get is dead silence. Suddenly, everybody in the room is confronted with things no one cares to reveal. Then, after the embarrassment subsides, you get a list of words such as the following: *law — judge — pleasure — sex — fault — death — parents — anger — forbidden,* and so on.

At the personal level, thinking about sin and guilt is not a neutral exercise. It involves us personally because it makes us aware that, little by little, we have woven for ourselves a way of life that includes both pleasures and prohibitions. It makes us remember how we have, or have not, accepted things forbidden by our parents — how we do or do not accept authority in all its forms.

The idea of sin also makes us think about our anxieties, our freedom, and the hidden desires we would rather not talk about. Ultimately, reflection on sin touches on two of the most important realities of life: *sexuality,* in a wide sense of the term, and *violence* or *aggression* — and, we might add: *death.*

This seems to be what advertisers understand when they use "sin" to sell their products. Besides the forbidden transgression involved, sin is often experienced as the fulfillment of a promised satisfaction: "It will make you happier!"

Sin takes us back to our search for pleasure. It prompts a person to ask questions like the following: What can I do to keep from indulging myself? Are the things I indulge in really sinful? Is God the kind of God who wants to keep us from being happy or free?

In the more serious moments of our lives, when we think about sin, these are the kinds of questions that occur to us.

Sin — A Key Topic for Christians

Sin is a key element in Scripture and Church Tradition. In the New Testament alone, the Greek word *hamartia,* which means sin, is found no less than 171 times. Besides *hamartia,* there are other words such as *anomia,* which means iniquity; *asebeia,* impiety; *adikia,* injustice; and finally *parabasis,* transgression. When we take all these words into account, we see that sin has a prominent place in the New Testament.

Sin is also a key element because of its importance in the mystery of salvation. The exposing of sin is at the heart of the revelation of Jesus Christ. In 1 Corinthians 15:3, one of the earliest faith-statements recorded in the New Testament, we read: *Christ died for our sins in accordance with the Scriptures.*

The word *sin* also appears in every Eucharistic celebration. At the moment the priest consecrates the wine, he says the following, based on the words of Jesus: *"This is the cup of my blood . . . it will be shed for you and for all so that sins may be forgiven."*

Finally, remember the words of Saint John:

If we say we have no sin, we deceive ourselves, and the truth is not in us. . . . If we say we have not sinned, we make him a liar, and his word is not in us. (1 John 1:8,10)

Sin is central to the revelation of Jesus Christ, and the place it holds in theological reflection is equally important. Let us begin our theological reflection by describing the shape and direction the sense of sin has taken in recent times.

CHAPTER 2

The Shift
in Our Sense of Sin

In recent times the sense of sin people have has undergone change at various levels. At the level of *everyday living,* you can hear remarks like the following: "When I go to confession I just can't figure out what my sins are anymore." One thing this means is that, for many people, "laundry lists" of sins no longer ring true. Even in well-prepared penance services the examination of conscience often grates on people.

On the level of *vocabulary,* we are also witnessing considerable change. For example, who uses the expression "mortal sin" anymore? Hardly anyone. When the Holy See used the term in *Persona Humana,* its 1976 declaration on sexual ethics, it was written up in the newspapers. Still, we might ask ourselves if there is not something in this expression worth preserving. Saint John, after all, speaks of sins that lead to death. And Saint Paul speaks of sins which exclude from the Kingdom. What is the meaning of our reluctance to face the idea of death linked to sin?

Lastly, there is an important change going on at the level of *the very notion of sin itself.* In order to understand this point better, let me describe, in very simplified terms, the past and present concepts of sin.

• *In the past,* the notion of sin was a weighty reality in our lives. We understood it in the context of the courtroom. We spoke of a divine judge and of sanctions.

Today, we have moved from that weighty, juridical concept of sin to a concept influenced by the nondirective approach. Little by little, dealing with sin has been put into the context of a ministry of mercy. The focus these days is on creating confidence rather than on fear. (Here we might ask ourselves what this blocking of fear out of our lives means. Fear, remember, is not all negative; it can stimulate attention and effort. I am not sure that excluding every trace of fear from catechetics and preaching does not also exclude something fundamental to human beings. This is a basic question that calls for reflection.) Confessors and spiritual directors often encourage penitents to confess their most important sins and faults, and to discern the roots of them. The truth is, many penitents no longer know very well what is important and what isn't.

• *In the past,* we thought of sin almost as a thing that had its own existence. We described it as something dirty, even contagious, and we talked about "the soul blackened by sin." You would hear confession referred to as something like a bath or a car wash.

Today, we have dropped the symbolism of sin as something defiling (and we may ask whether that was such a good idea). In its place we have a concept of sin that is purely *relational.* Sin is no longer seen as a stain but as an injury done to another. So, instead of talking about purification, we refer to confession as the Sacrament of Reconciliation.

• *In the past,* our concept of sin was much more *individual.* Apart from deliberately missing Mass on Sunday or eating meat on Friday, the sins that counted as mortal were mainly of a sexual and private nature. Most of the other mortal sins — murder, serious theft, and so on — were simply not problems for the average Christian. In confession, that narrowed the field down pretty much to sexual sins.

Today, in contrast to that very individualistic view, we have a very *collective* concept of sin — perhaps excessively collective, because a sin that is everyone's is a sin that is no one's. The emphasis today is no longer on sexual sins but on the sin of individualism and fatalism: the refusal to participate in making history and building a better world. The disorder emphasized today is not so much in the individual's heart and emotions but in the political, economic, and social order.

• *In the past,* we had a *legalistic* concept of sin. For example, *The Maryknoll Catholic Dictionary,* published in 1965, defines sin as a "deliberate transgression against the law of God." The 1969 edition of the *Saint Joseph Baltimore Catechism* says: "Actual sin is any willful thought, desire, word, action, or omission forbidden by the law of God."

Today, we have a more *mystical* concept: sin is a refusal to follow the call of Christ. We speak very little about *law,* even "the law of Christ," despite the fact that this expression is from Saint Paul (see 1 Corinthians 9:21 and Galatians 6:2).

• Curiously enough, this more legalistic concept *of the past* was ultimately linked to a truly God-centered concept — sin as an offense against God. It said that sin touches God and that the primary reason we are to avoid sin is because it is an injury to God's glory. We had a legalistic concept, but one that ended up being God-centered.

Today, we have a mystical concept (sin as refusing the call of Christ), which may be going overboard by viewing sin as nothing more than an injury to another human being. There is so much stress on the human that many people wonder whether sin has anything at all to do with God.

These, I think, are some of the main trends in the shift we have witnessed in recent times. Let us now try to understand the causes.

CHAPTER 3

Some Causes
of the Shift

The Human Sciences

The impact of Marxist thought. For the sake of convenience, I am including Marxist thought under the human sciences, even though there are contemporary thinkers who would seriously question my doing so. My reason for including it here is that the thought of Marx and his followers has profoundly influenced the understanding of sin in many countries with Christian populations.

According to Marxists, morality is that cluster of precepts to which the individual must submit. The dominant morality is always an ideological product of the economic infrastructure at a given epoch in history.

According to the Marxists, the key characteristic of Christian morality is that it passes itself off as being rooted in the Word of God; it is supposed to come straight from the Gospel. But in fact, Marxists say, Christian morality is often at the service of the dominant capitalist class.

Furthermore, according to certain Marxists, the concept of sin seems to allow economic structures that cause alienation to go unquestioned. (*Alienation* means a condition of basic disrespect for human dignity, in which people treat others, and themselves, as things. Marx held that the drive toward "having things" prevents us from "being ourselves" and makes us *aliens* in our own world.) The idea of sin does this because it tends to channel questions of conduct to private conscience, thus tending to make us view matters only from their private side. Meanwhile, say Marxists, the true causes of alienation are so deeply social that the concept of sin tends to promote passive resignation in the face of exploitation. Marxists claim that Christian guilt focuses on two dominant themes — disobedience to authority and sexual impurity.

As regards authority, it is Saint Paul who wrote: *"Let every person be subject to the governing authorities. For there is no authority except from God, and those that exist have been instituted by God."* (Romans 13:1) This statement, taken out of context, always aggravates Marxists, who see in it the seeds of resignation to all established disorders, and to all powers, even the most dictatorial.

Then there is sexuality. In this area, Marxists say, emphasis on guilt seems to cause a person to focus too much on self, thereby leading the person to accept excessive control of society over the individual.

Faced with all the questioning that is going on, many Christians have found themselves quite uncomfortable. By way of reaction, some have tended to insist stridently on collective guilt and to harbor suspicion about the existence of personal sin.

Psychoanalytic thought. It is out of the question here to treat the psychoanalytic critique in detail. What I will do is highlight some of the points raised by psychoanalysis regarding the concept of sin.

First of all, from the Freudian perspective it has been shown that all behavior amounts to a formation resulting from compromise between external reality and the demands of the unconscious. Human behavior is thus perceived as a set of symptoms whose hidden meaning needs to be sought. For example, masturbation, homosexuality, marital conflicts — such things are perceived not primarily as expressions of sin but as expressions of a "deeper" psychic reality. They are symptoms that need to be explored if we are to get at their roots. This view leads some people to ask what is the point of talking about sin in terms of rules of morality.

Doesn't that prevent us from discerning the unconscious roots of behavior?

A second issue is the definite impact psychoanalytic trends have had on how Christians relate to sexuality, which has long been an important area of guilt.

A third issue is the doubt psychoanalysis has sown about the extent of our psychological freedom. Are we really free? In certain places in his writings, Freud goes so far as to say that human beings are determined by their impulses.

A fourth issue is the psychoanalytic tenet that all confession is more or less an exercise in narcissism. From that viewpoint, examinations of conscience and the practice of confession are objects of suspicion.

A fifth issue is the psychoanalytic finding that guilt is rooted in our childhood past. Thus, psychoanalyst Melanie Klein says that our guilt feelings originate at age two in our relationship to our mother. "Well, then," people say to themselves, "doesn't this mean that what we call sin is just an outmoded prolonging of old psychological problems?" This line of questioning has gone so far that some psychiatrists suspect Christians of having a specific neurosis.

Finally, as a result of these trends, psychoanalysis favors the nondirective approach which, in the United States, is associated with the name of Carl Rogers. To many pastors and religious educators, this nonjudgmental and open acceptance of people who unburden themselves seems to be a more constructive approach than focusing on people's ethical failings and urging them on to self-improvement.

All of these factors engender an attitude of cautiousness in the way sin is talked about.

The new epistemology. Epistemology, as you know, studies human knowing. Contemporary epistemology has emphasized reflection on the various sciences. What impact does contemporary epistemology have on the theme of sin?

1. Edgard Morin, a great contemporary French thinker, writes: "At the heart of each of us there is ambiguity and antagonism." What this means is that no human act ever has effects that we can be sure are purely humanizing or de-

humanizing. All human acts have multiple long-term and short-term effects, some of which are contradictory.

Take the 1980 workers' strike in Poland, for example. This strike had very positive consequences; it represented a step toward freedom for a relatively oppressed people. But the strike also had negative consequences: a destabilized economy, acute risk of invasion by a foreign country, and so on.

In a totally different context, the liturgy gives the name *felix culpa* — happy fault — to a particularly dehumanizing act: the sin that led ultimately to the death of Jesus on the Cross. And yet, out of this dehumanizing act good things resulted.

Awareness of the ambiguity of our acts makes it more difficult at times to tell whether the good or the evil predominates. Though there may be some human acts that have no apparent good effect, judging the goodness or evil of an act often comes down to judging which effects predominate. When I say that this behavior is good or is evil, I am taking a linguistic shortcut. To be exact, I should say that such behavior gives rise to dominant effects that tend to be good or humanizing — or to dominant effects that tend to be alienating or dehumanizing.

These considerations call to mind the very important Gospel parable of the good seed and the bad (Matthew 13:24-30). This parable can help us appreciate the ambiguities in our acts and transgressions. The fact that an act has some positive consequences can make it difficult for us to see that it is also sinful, with negative consequences.

2. A second lesson that becomes apparent from examining contemporary science is this: every reality exists at the heart of a *system,* a network of elements which have complex interactions between them.

To illustrate what I mean, let us look at the medical-moral issue of prolonging life. Some medical personnel seem convinced that any medical treatment — no matter how unproven or expensive — must be used to prolong a dying person's life, as if the medical-technical reality were the only factor involved. On the other hand, some religious people refuse any medical treatment whatsoever and place absolute trust in the healing power of God, as if all technological developments were evil. The truth is that contemporary human beings live in a complex social system where high-tech medical developments must be weighed in the context of basic human values. The medical system exists to serve the human person, who lives within a system called the family, which exists within a larger system called society. All of these complex factors, and the interactions between them, need to be weighed in judging the moral obligation to prolong life.

Leaving that example aside, and moving to a larger context, it must be affirmed that there is no possibility of grasping the significance of an act without taking into account the other realities with which the act forms a system. Thus the immense complexity of the interpretive process that goes into declaring this or that behavior sinful or not.

3. One final remark about epistemology:

Reflection on the human sciences teaches us that the actions of a subject exist only in the context of the subject's *history*. Hence the need to know the past history of a subject in judging responsibility. An area in which this applies is adolescent sexual transgressions. Consider the case of an adolescent boy who has had sexual relations with a girl. If we focus only on the objective act itself — "grave matter," according to the catechism definition — it is easy to say: That is a sin. But once we focus on the subject and his personal development, we see other factors to be weighed. For example, the young person's transgression might have been part of a struggle on his part to discover the opposite sex. It also might have been a very selfish search for pleasure. It also might have been an effort to prove to himself that he is sexually "normal." It also might have been an expression of escape from parental control by doing something forbidden.

It is not difficult to judge the objective morality of the act. But once sensitivity is brought to bear on a youth's personal development, the discernment process about subjective guilt is neither simple nor easy.

Sociological Factors

Given the limitation of space here, I will be very brief. First, let us focus on the problems that are suddenly impacting us on a global scale. In only a few decades our planet has become a "global village." As a result, it has become difficult to sort out our priorities and responsibilities. Take, for example, the problem of helping an underdeveloped country controlled by a murderous dictator. Is it more moral to send aid to that country, when you know that the dictator might use the aid for his own purposes? Or is it more moral to send nothing, thus contributing to the dictator's downfall by allowing the national economy to collapse?

The global sweep of such problems often leaves average Christians with the impression that they are relieved of their ethical responsibilities; with the impression that, after all, only a few executives in multinational corporations know what is really going on — if even they do! No wonder it is difficult to internalize what collective sin means.

To conclude this brief reflection on the impact that social factors are having on the notion of sin, let me mention two final influences. First, the influence of the media. The media — TV, films, etcetera — are flooding us with a bewildering variety of ethical viewpoints. This is the case in areas such as respect for life, abortion, divorce, and juvenile cohabitation.

Second, there is widespread *unbelief,* clearly a key cause of the loss of the sense of sin. As I will point out later, there is no true sense of sin except in relation to God.

These, then, are a few of the reasons why uneasiness about sin has taken hold today. Other factors could easily be mentioned. In the realm of theology, for example, the emphasis in recent years on the Spirit rather than on the law-making Father coincides with a de-emphasis on sin. It is easy to see, I think, that these influences go deep. Christians are going to need time to regain confidence in their understanding of sin and in dealing with guilt.

PART TWO

THE ORIGINAL SIN

What I would like to do, using some tools borrowed from psychoanalysis, is to take a fresh look at what can be called a sin-type, the sin described in chapter 3 of the Book of Genesis. This will help us to see what the "beginning" of sin (temptation) is, what sin itself is, and what its consequences are.

The narrative of Adam's transgression in Saint Paul's letters and in tradition is closely related to the doctrine of original sin. In view of this fact, I will conclude Part Two by making a few brief observations on what is meant by "original sin."

CHAPTER 4

Opening Remarks About Genesis 3

1. We should take notice, first of all, that the act described in Genesis 3 is not called a "fall." It is important to emphasize this fact because the word *fall* conjures up the idea of falling from an extraordinary, "supra-natural" state to a lesser, merely natural state. It is better to speak of Genesis 3 as the narrative of a transgression, because the human beings in Genesis 3 were not endowed with extraordinary gifts.

2. The narrative of the sin of Adam and Eve is not often mentioned in Scripture. The Old Testament refers to it only twice — Sirach 25:24 and Wisdom 2:24. As for the New Testament, we must distinguish between the Gospels and the Pauline writings. In the Gospels, Jesus does not explicitly refer to the transgression narrative except possibly in John 8:44. In contrast, Paul attaches great importance to Adam's transgression. Why? Because Paul is sensitive to the solidarity of all human beings in the salvation brought by Christ, the new Man, the new Adam. But Paul also points out our solidarity in sin due to the sin of Adam. In other words — and this is a key point — it is Christology that gave rise to reflection on Adam, to what theologians call Adamology.

3. Most biblical scholars agree that in the Book of Genesis there are three literary traditions: the Yahwist, Elohist, and

Priestly sources. The transgression narrative is from the Yahwist tradition, which dates back to the 950s before Christ. The literary genre of this narrative is *mythical,* in the noblest sense of the term. As dictionaries point out, the word *myth* applies to traditional stories, parables, and allegories. In calling the transgression narrative mythical, we do not mean that it is imaginary nonsense. We mean that the narrative communicates truth, but does so by way of symbol or metaphor. The transgression narrative does not, and was never intended to, describe an actual historical event.

What this basically means, as Paul Ricoeur has explained so well, is that the narrative seeks to "concretize the universal" or to *universalize human experience.* "Mister Adam" is Mister Everybody. This is why everyone can find in it something of his or her own experience when this text is read today, almost 3,000 years after it was put in final form.

Finally, when we bear in mind the human condition in which we find ourselves, the myth is a source for endless reflection on the unfolding of our own history.

4. This narrative probably has an etiological function. That is, it seeks to reflect on the origin of evil or the things that go wrong in human history. We all know that the problem of evil is a major human problem — "the principal stimulus for reflection and the most cunning invitation for irrational talk," as Ricoeur puts it. Evil confronts us with absurdity, and contact with it always gives rise to two questions: Where does it come from? Why does it exist?

Religious thought has always been preoccupied with this piercing question, and it has responded in different ways. To give a better understanding of the originality of Christian thought, let me point out four classic answers found in the history of religions.

— Some schools of religious thought say that the origin of evil is coextensive with the origin of things and is to be found in the primordial chaos. Salvation consists in the act of a good God who struggles against this chaos in order to establish his creation.

— Other religions and myths state that we have the kind of God who instigates temptation, a God who blinds and leads astray, who submits human beings to a tragic destiny against which they are helpless. This kind of thought has come down to us mainly in the Greek tragedies.

— Some religions have claimed that there are two principles of creation: a god of goodness and a god of evil.

— Other religions, finally, locate the origin of evil in the downfall of souls — sparks of the divine — into matter. The body is therefore seen as an evil structure which encloses man from the outside. Evil is ultimately the very worldliness of the world. In this line of thought, man is not truly responsible for evil, even though he is its carrier.

Seen in the light of these religious attempts at explanation, the narrative of Adam's transgression is also an effort, that of the Jewish faith, to reflect on the basic question of the origin of evil and of good. The great axis — the point around which the narrative hinges — is that it separates the origin of good and evil into two:

— On the one hand, it affirms that before all clse there is the origin of good — God — who brings into being a good creation.

— On the other hand, it affirms that evil finds its radical origin *partly* in the free transgression of one of God's commandments by a human couple, the couple itself being the result of a creative act by God. I say *partly* because Adam and Eve, as we shall see, are going to find themselves confronted by the serpent who has already perverted the Word of God before they come on the scene (see Paul Ricoeur, *The Symbolism of Evil,* Beacon Press, pages 252-260).

Thus, in the Bible, evil is in part a reality for which human beings are responsible — we are not its helpless pawns. In contrast, many of the other myths present evil as something that contaminates human beings in spite of themselves. In chapter 3 of Genesis, the human being is presented as guilty, as responsible for certain bad relationships and historical happenings. Seen in this light, the biblical myth has a foundational perspective for ethical reflection. It asserts that human beings are not marionettes manipulated by evil forces. They are free, capable in part of determining their own destinies.

Before we go on to put the transgression narrative in its proper context (the creation story of chapter 2 in Genesis), I would like to present a few points, in layman's terms, from psychoanalysis. This will enable us to see some of the human richness in the narratives of Genesis 2 and 3. This in turn will unveil some extraordinary parallels between contemporary anthropological findings and the perspectives contained in the biblical narratives.

In case any readers view this as an attempt to turn the Bible into a science textbook, I want to state that I make no claim that the biblical creation narrative provides, or tries to provide, a scientific description of the appearance of human life on earth. Nor do I claim that the Bible pioneered psychoanalysis. These parallels between contemporary research and mythical expressions are meant simply to show that, as I see it, the Word of God is spoken and grasps us through the most basic structures of our humanity.

CHAPTER 5

Human Birthing —
A Psychoanalytic Focus

In the mother's womb every human being is, to use the Latin word, *infans* — unable to speak. The infant lies in the undifferentiated world of the self, represented by the egg shape in the diagram on the next page. This world of the womb is often called *fusional* because life in it is a total sharing between infant and mother. This fusional world leaves its imprint on the human person; its traces are present throughout life.

The most important characteristic of this original world is *undifferentiation*. In this womb world there is no awareness of the two great differences in the world outside: *time*, which marks all our lives, and the presence of the *other*, with which we must be in contact simply to live.

Another feature of this fusional world is that there is *no mediation* in it — no "other" that could make the infant aware of otherness.

This is also a world without failure — especially the two great failures we experience in life: the failure of defeat and the radical failure of death.

The infant has yet to know the other. It lives in a pure realm of the self, a world of identity and sameness. It never occurs to the infant that anything could even exist that might resist its power. And so the infant lives in a world characterized by a *dream* of *omnipotence*.

This is the original world we came from, and its traces remain all our lives. It is a world for which we will always have a certain nostalgia, no matter how old we get. It is a wonderful world to live in, but it has one drawback: to live in that world means being shut out of this other, real world. The process of becoming a human subject entails being willing to *let go* of that fusional world *in order to find* the Other in its otherness.

So it is that, even at the start, there is a resurrection structure to life — a dying to one life and a finding of a new one. We have to let go in order to find.

The speechless *infans* must leave its primitive fusion in order to be able to speak, communicate, and love. To live will always mean to articulate the memories of the *Self* that dwell within and to meet the *Other* who awaits and forms us.

The infant does not leave its wonder world by its own power. And being brought forth from the womb is not enough to bring about the letting go. The infant has to be made to understand deep down that from now on it is impossible — and forbidden — to return to that wondrous existence it thought would never end.

The thing that disillusions the infant, that forces it to let go of its womb world, is a prohibition: *Undifferentiation is no longer permitted.* As we see in the diagram, this prohibition establishes a decisive gap between the infant and its original existence. From now on, there is to be no more world without differences and failures, no more world in which self is all-powerful.

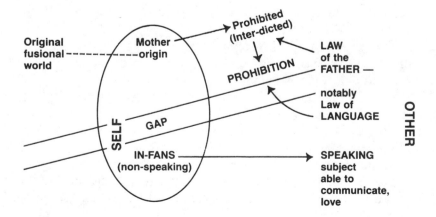

The diagram shows why a prohibition is needed to call the person forth. The prohibition is life-giving because it prevents the person from coinciding or merging with its own self or with the other. Concretely, this means that in human relations there are always three dimensions involved: the other, myself, and the gap. What it amounts to is the end of the dream of being all-knowing, of having total knowledge of one's world.

What is the brunt of the life-giving prohibition? It is what psychoanalysis terms "the law of the father." This is not just the law of the flesh-and-blood daddy; it encompasses a much broader reality. The law of the father is the law of culture and especially the law of language, which is both a medium and a buffer between us and the realities our words express. Speaking always stakes out distances between oneself and the things one gives names to. To speak about a thing means that the speaker no longer coincides with, no longer has a sense of sameness with, that thing. Speech establishes and recognizes the existence of the gap.

To put this another way, these nontechnical expressions of psychoanalytic thought are saying that meaningful living demands that we take differences into account, that we deny ourselves omnipotence and coincidence or fusion with the other, that we embrace the cultural realities which put us in touch with, and at a distance from, our world.

Now we are going to see that the mythic narratives of chapters 2 and 3 in the Book of Genesis present some extraordinary *analogies* with these contemporary anthropological findings, as well as some corollaries about what it means to be human in the presence of God.

CHAPTER 6

The Creation Story — Genesis 2

The creation narrative in Genesis 2:46–3:24 depicts the world in its original state as a barren desert. It describes the passage from rough, uncultivated nature to human culture through the *mediation* of human labor (verse 2:15).

Creation develops to the point where there is human language: "The man gave names to all cattle, and to the birds of the air, and to every beast of the field . . . " (verse 20a).

So, we see man, from the start, performing an act of creation by giving names. But this narrative of creation does not stop with naming animals. It culminates in man's articulate, jubilant cry when he recognizes woman as his true counterpart: "This at last is bone of my bones and flesh of my flesh; she shall be called Woman *[Ishsha],* because she was taken out of Man *[Ish]*" (verse 2:23).

So, according to the author, God's creative act is one that allows a world where animate and inanimate beings are subject to the power of the human person, a subjection brought about by the mediation of work and language.

Finally, notice from now on that the height of the creative act is the joyful acknowledgment of the difference between the sexes.

But let us read the text more closely. The narrative begins with a description of a land without trees or plants. Only subterranean waters seep through to the surface (verse 2:4-6d). This land is a desert because man is not there to cultivate it. At this point, Yahweh appears on the scene like a potter to do a job of modeling (verse 2:7a). With dust taken from the ground *(adama)* Adam is fashioned. This part of verse 7 brings out two points:

First, God is a unique kind of potter. He uses dust *(aphar)* and not clay to fashion Adam.

Second, the man — who, we later learn, is endowed with sexuality — is presented to us as being in kinship with the cosmos, and in its most ordinary guise: dust — dust that sticks to the soles of our feet, dust that we try to shake off. This point alone invites reflection on our deep cosmic roots — roots to which animals have equal claim (verse 2:19). Even in adult life these obscure cosmic origins always color our desires. Genuine respect for creation never opts for eliminating or denying these forces at work in us, even though they sometimes beckon us to regress.

Verse 7b shows how God gives life to this form he has modeled: God blows into the man's nostrils a breath of life *(neshama)*. This *neshama* surely symbolizes human frailty, especially the human power of self-determination that has its source in the Creator. It is true *self-determination* because the man now breathes on his own. Notice, for example, how a tiny infant has far greater autonomy in breathing than in taking nourishment. Still, this power has its roots in the Creator; in the creation story it is God who decides to communicate his breath to inanimate human nature.

Notice too that this same God-rooted self-determination is found again in the culmination of God's re-creative activity represented by Pentecost (Acts of the Apostles, chapter 2). The early Christian community is re-created — given new life — by receiving the breath *(pneuma)* of Jesus. To be life-giving, Scripture tells us, all moral striving toward humanization needs to go from being a body alive by the breath of Yahweh (Genesis 2:7) to a body alive in the *pneuma* (1 Corinthians, chapter 6), a body ultimately destined to become a totally "pneumatic" — spiritual — body (1 Corinthians 15:44).

Here we glimpse the wealth of meaning in the breath *(Ruah)* that moved "over the face of the waters" in Genesis 1:2, the breath which Luke 1:35 says came upon Mary to bring forth the firstborn of the new creation.

Thinking about flesh-and-blood people and their human relationships can bring one back to thinking about the body into which God breathed life and about the breath of the Creator. The Gospel of John tells us this is the only breath that can guide us into the truth (John 16:13); to sin against it is to condemn oneself to being forever unable to meet God (Matthew 12:32).

Verses 2:8 and 2:15 show us that God puts the first man into the Garden of Eden to transform the earth by his *labor.* It is interesting that in this garden of delights, where life seems quite pleasant, the man meets up with the *mediations* required for cultivating the earth. According to the author, living happily does not mean living without mediations as one would in the fusional world of the womb.

This point is addressed indirectly in the Gospel of Luke. There the devil suggests that Jesus use his power as Son of God to waive the mediation of work: "If you are the Son of God, command this stone to become bread." (Luke 4:3) Jesus flatly refuses to exercise this kind of omnipotence.

The refusal of instant gratification is accentuated even more forcefully in Genesis 2 by use of what we might call a basic prohibition (verses 9 and 16-17). Quite remarkably, this prohibition essentially focuses on an oral function: " . . . of the tree of the knowledge of good and evil you shall not eat. . . . " This function is at the root of the most archaic, primal structures of the personality; it is not surprising that, in the Bible, temptations are very often oral ones — for example, the temptation of the first couple, the temptation of God's people in the desert, and the temptation of Jesus. By this prohibition God challenges the man's desire; from now on human beings will not be able to eat the fruit of the tree of knowledge.

Chapter 2 in Genesis tells us that to love and to live well means to work; it means to desire in a world marked by differences — between trees permitted and forbidden — and by the gap.

Notice also that verse 2:9 introduces the theme of sight: "And out of the ground the LORD God made to grow every tree that is pleasant to the sight. ... " Sight here simply means a source of enjoyment. But in chapter 3 it will play a key role as an opening through which temptation makes its entry.

The basic prohibition laid down by God is accompanied by a declaration in verse 17: " ... the day that you eat of it you shall die." Is this to be taken as a divine threat? Is God saying, "If you disobey I will punish you"?

If that were the case, the threat would be about an extrinsic punishment rather than a warning about an effect that would be an outgrowth from the man's attitude and behavior. Looking at the rest of the narrative, we see that Adam and Eve do not in fact die immediately after the transgression. And in verse 3:19 God tells Adam, "you are dust and to dust you shall return." These passages, plus other places in the Bible that view death as a natural phenomenon, lead many theologians not to adopt the divine threat interpretation. A number of them favor reading verse 17 as a declaration that bears itself out. It would go like this: "A life worth living is possible only for the person who respects the gap, mediations, and the inability to be all-knowing about good and evil. If these boundaries to human desire are not respected, then — by internal necessity — death is the only outcome the desiring subject can expect at the end of the road."

Notice that the forbidden fruit is from the tree of the knowledge of good and evil. Scripture scholars say that this tree bears fruit that gives mastery over secrets that are beyond human grasp. God "castrates" man for wanting to know everything, wanting to control everything. The salvation of the human person lies in having gnosis — "higher knowledge" — denied him. Salvation lies in the prohibition of omniscience.

After this description of the human being subjected to the basic prohibition and marked by desire, verse 2:18 takes note of the man's aloneness: "it is not good that the man should be alone; I will make him a helper fit for him." Solitude is presented here in its distressing form — loneliness. The man's desire cannot find its life's fulfillment until he has the companionship of the woman. The transgression narrative also implies that one of the effects of sin is that it returns us to the loneliness of guilt which tends to cut us off from others (Genesis 3:12). Verses 2:19 and 2:20 describe Yahweh forming the animals, like the man, from the earth. But notice that Genesis does not say that these animals receive God's breath of life *(neshama)*. Though the animals are creatures too, it is as if the man's likeness to them is too weak. Here we find a very pertinent law of psychology: too great a difference always plunges one into loneliness. Only a good articulation of differences and likenesses, of the other and the self, allows us to feel at home in the human condition. This very point helps us to grasp the meaning of the creation of the woman from "the rib which the LORD God had taken from the man." This narrative brings home the fact that the woman is both very similar to and very different from the man. Man and woman are shown as having the same nature, of being made of the same flesh. The man's jubilant cry says it all: "This at last is bone of my bones and flesh of my flesh. . . . "

Notice that this communion of man and woman does not originate from the man's initiative. Here again all that Adam does is recognize a reality that does not depend on him. In fact, its origin is partly hidden from him because the creation of the woman took place while Adam was in a deep sleep. So once again the narrative hits upon a form of unknowing. The relentless desire to know everything — to be almighty, to know all about where we and everyone else come from — ends up in frustration. It is in this state of unknowing that the man's first words manage to capture the likeness-unlikeness of the woman. Because she is taken from man, *Ish,* she is called wo-man, *Ishsha.*

And so we end up seeing that, according to these biblical narratives, God's creative activity brings forth not a supra-natural world but a world in which human beings take charge through the mediation of work and language. It is a world in which differences — between permitted and forbidden trees, between God and creatures, between man and woman — are recognized in the context of faith in the prohibiting word of the Creator. Lastly, it is a world where there can be joyous moments of intimate union without regression into the natural world from which humanity has emerged. The transgression narrative helps us to be aware of how human sin leads to a thorough breakdown of this balance of life, to a kind of de-creation.

CHAPTER 7

The Transgression Story — Genesis 3

The narrative of the original sin begins by pointing out, in verse 2:25, that the man and the woman are naked without feeling any shame. The Church has a long history of exploring this sexual theme in the sin narrative. With a little help from the unconscious, some theologians have gone so far as to say that the original sin was a sexual sin. The reading we just did of the creation narrative avoids that kind of speculation.

How, then, are we to understand this theme of nakedness? First of all, we should note that nakedness immediately connotes weakness — a naked person is a vulnerable person. It is deeply significant that the New Testament presents Jesus — the New Adam, perfectly innocent, perfectly responsive to God — dying naked on a cross, with nothing but the power of his Father to trust in.

But it seems to me that we can see this theme of nakedness from yet another approach. Chapter 2 in Genesis presents the man and the woman living without shame in each other's presence, unclothed. What this may mean is that they are conscious of their sexual differences and mutual dependence. This difference and dependence bring home to them their non-Almighty-ness — the stark fact of their creatureliness. As any one of us can easily testify, sex is one of those areas in which we experience our dependence and limitations. Sexuality makes it clear to us that we are drawn toward the other, that we are not the be-all of humanity.

Being a man makes one realize that one cannot be a woman — and vice versa.

Adam and Eve are good at living with limitations, verse 25 tells us. But life is still a challenge because it sets boundaries to the desire for omnipotence. So, all it takes is a trifle to turn this challenge into a temptation to sin. This trifle is introduced by that most cunning of animals, the serpent. Just as Satan does with Jesus in Luke 4, the serpent in Genesis 3 dangles a captivating lure before the eyes of the man and the woman. This lure is like a beckoning promise, a siren song, rising out of the lingering traces of the fusional womb world we once inhabited.

The serpent first approaches the woman. Many people have wondered, Why the woman first? Why not Adam? Some see evidence here of the male chauvinism that permeated the society in which the author wrote. That could be part of it — but I think we hit closer to home by seeing here a logic inherent in the narrative itself. The narrative portrays the woman as the high point of God's creative act; the process reaches completion with the creation of Eve. After that, the transgression brings about a de-creation. In this light, it makes sense for the de-creation to begin with the summit of creation — the woman — so as to make its impact bit by bit on the rest of the world God created.

Having approached the woman, the serpent tries to entice her to transgress. He does this by distorting God's basic prohibition, giving it an expanded scope that the Creator had not intended: "Did God say, 'You shall not eat of *any* tree of the garden'?" (verse 3:1b) Here the serpent is insinuating that the God who creates desire is a dreadful, castrating God who allows no desire whatsoever to find fulfillment. (Aren't *all* trees forbidden?)

This temptation of Eve by the serpent strikes me as a temptation I find repeatedly in my pastoral experience. How many times I have found myself with good people overtaken by a sense of being stifled by a castrating God. They say things like, "God created me with sexual desires, desires to possess things, desires to take control, to be assertive . . . but God keeps me from being that way. The Gospel says, 'Be meek, love your enemies, turn your cheek,' and all the rest. God is sadistic! He created me with all these desires and then he keeps me from fulfilling them."

In statements like these, you can spot the serpent's whole strategy. He expands God's prohibitions. So often temptation gets through to people by presenting prohibitions blown all *out of proportion*. The truth is that God has never forbidden the use of sex or power or money or aggressiveness. God simply asks that, for our own good, we not misuse sex, power, money, and aggressiveness.

But back to the narrative. Faced with the serpent's insinuations, the woman begins to give in to the maneuver being used on her. Now she too expands the divine prohibitions. She says, " . . . God said, 'You shall not eat of the fruit of the tree which is in the midst of the garden, neither shall you *touch* it . . . ' " (verse 3:3). As a matter of fact, touching the fruit had not been forbidden by God (verse 2:17). What we see in Eve's reaction here is a classic psychological rule: when a person experiences a desire to transgress, the person tends to accentuate the prohibition in an attempt to avoid the transgression. This is a twisted way we have of protecting ourselves from ourselves. The problem is, by not facing into our desires more honestly right on the spot, we risk getting to a point someday where we have a transgression on our hands that goes farther than we ever wanted.

The woman is now ready to disregard the serious consequences of God's prohibitions. "You will not die," says the serpent. "For God knows that when you eat of [the fruit] your eyes will be opened, and you will be like God, knowing good and evil." We see that the serpent has understood an essential fact — that all sin begins with inattention to the Word of God. The serpent proposes that the woman give up trusting in the Word of the Creator and open her eyes. What we see here is a temptation that comes up repeatedly in the Bible — the temptation to go beyond *believing* in the Word to *seeing*.

Belief implies that we trust a person's word about something we have no personal knowledge of. To trust only in what we see means wanting something we can "get a handle on." We can understand why the Gospel of John declares, "Blessed are those who have not seen and yet believe," and associates faith with seeing on the occasion when the disciples arrive at Jesus' tomb and find it . . . empty (John 20:29 and 20:8). It is also worth remarking that the transgression narrative associates the promise of seeing all with knowing all — in other words, with total control over prohibitions.

"... *your eyes will be opened, and you will be like God....*" Here is the promise of divine omnipotence all over again. Satan suggests that the human being leave the human condition behind in order to attain a superhuman — and therefore an inhuman — state of pseudodivinity. Jesus, the Son of God, will reverse this insatiable quest of sinful humanity by taking on the human condition out of love, even to the point of dying in solidarity with those whom society looks down on (Luke 4:1-13; Philippians 2:6-11). And Jesus will explicitly recall this reversal of things to the disciples on the road to Emmaus (Luke 24:26).

The woman finally gives in to the temptation to eat, and she uses her solidarity with the man to draw him into rejecting faith in God's Word. Then their eyes are opened (verse 7). But what they see is how limited the human condition is, how impossible it is to fulfill the promises of the primal world they lived in: " . . . they knew that they were naked." Transgressing the prohibition was supposed to open their eyes to their own omnipotence. Instead, what they see is that differences exist.

This may be what the part about nakedness in the transgression narrative is getting at. As we mentioned before, a person who is conscious of being naked in front of the opposite sex is a person who is aware of the marked sexual difference in bodily appearance. As long as they accepted God's prohibition, the man and the woman were comfortable with this difference (Genesis 2:25). But as soon as they transgressed, even though the sin focused their attention on their sexual difference, they immediately started acting as if the difference did not exist. This is one way of reading verse 7b: " . . . they sewed fig leaves together and made themselves aprons." It is as if the difference in sex could be blotted out by covering it up! "We are well aware," the first couple were saying, "that there is a difference between the sexes. But it reminds us of how limited we are. So let's cover it up."

And so it goes. Just like the first couple, the sinner in each of us says: "*I am well aware* of human limitation. It is only too real to me. *Still,* it has to be possible to become God. And if that isn't possible, I'll just have to cover up the fact that I'm so limited."

As an aside, it may be of interest to note that this opening of the eyes in the transgression narrative is found in another well-known Scripture narrative, the story of the disciples on the road to Emmaus in Luke 24. They, too, had been wrapped up in a dream of omnipotence because they thought Jesus would make everything bright and rosy by some kind of magic. Then it turned out that Jesus had to face death and failure. But then, behold, Jesus appears to them. He gives them a running commentary on the law and the prophets, reminding them of the divine prohibition which forces every human being to face his or her limitedness. Only then, after getting their attention back on the Word of God, does Jesus suggest that they eat something, as Satan had suggested eating. But instead of making eating an occasion for transgressing God's prohibition, Jesus makes it an occasion for the Emmaus disciples to make contact with the kingdom of God. This is why the disciples' eyes are opened during the meal with Jesus — opened to the radical difference between God and humanity. Carrying the point further, Christ immediately frustrates their sight by disappearing. Here, once again, sight is associated with recognizing the gap in order to give full scope to the act of believing.

Let us bring this commentary on the transgression narrative to a close by looking at the consequences of the sin.

The sin of Adam and Eve blurs the lines between difference and likeness. As a result, all of the areas in which difference ought to play a part are flawed by sin. Once they sin, Adam and Eve do a poor job of handling the difference between God and themselves because they fear God (Genesis 3:8). It will take a complete reeducation to get human beings to see that "perfect love casts out fear" (1 John 4:18).

After the sin, the man-woman difference goes badly. Here again the logic of the narrative is interesting. The woman was brought forth from Adam's side — from within the man. But from now on the sin distorts that connection; verse 3:16 says that the woman will have to submit to male domination and undergo hardship because of those whom she herself brings forth — her children.

The man came out of the ground. But as verse 3:17 shows, the man's relation to the earth turns out badly; after the sin he has to toil in pain to wrest a living from the earth.

The sin was a true breakdown of the world, a de-creation. That is why, in one fell swoop, sin does injury to God, to humanity, and to the cosmos.

CHAPTER 8

Genesis 2 and 3 —
A Summing Up

— All sin begins with inattention to the Word of God. We saw a good example of this in Eve's attitude to the proposals put forth by the serpent. This is why the New Testament urges: "Watch and pray that you may not enter into temptation. . . ." (Matthew 26:41) To pray means to keep ever in mind the unique things God has done. To watch means to keep ready to receive the Word.

— Sin often has its origin in a distortion of God's plan — that is, in a lie. Saint John goes so far as to call the devil "a liar and the father of lies" (John 8:44). As we already saw, falling for the lie that God wants to stifle our lives always leads to transgressing, when the truth is that God wants us to live.

— Sin is an act that always short-circuits the use of human mediations. We see this clearly in the three temptations of Jesus in chapter 4 of Luke. The first temptation consists in doing away with the mediation of work to obtain bread. The second does away with the mediation of time; Satan invites Jesus to acquire everything his heart desires right on the spot by worshiping Satan. And the third temptation proposes doing away with death and failure; Satan tells Jesus he won't kill himself if he throws himself off the pinnacle of the temple. These three temptations are variations of the dream we all have of recovering that original world we described in the egg diagram.

— Ultimately, all sin is like a will to tear down creation — a determined effort to change the other instead of respecting the other's difference, an attempt to regress to the state of undifferentiation. The result is a world whose harmony is shattered. Therein lies one source of the things in this world that go wrong and bring suffering. That is why sin always brings death into our midst. It does not always result in biological death. But it always results in some form of death to human relationships. This is why sin affects God's design, his desire to see us live life to the full.

— Every sin is an effort to throw off our condition as creatures and a quest for ultimate power. The sad part is that even the Word of God can sometimes be used perversely in the quest for omnipotence. We see a good case of this in the temptations of Jesus in Luke 4, where Satan uses the Word of God in Psalm 91 to try to get Jesus to go around his human limitations, notably the limitation of death.

— If the narrative in Genesis 2 and 3 is to be believed, temptation finds fertile ground for itself in the primal tendencies that dwell within us — especially in three desires we have:
First, there is the *oral* desire to consume. This is something to think about, especially in view of the fact that advertisers would have us believe that happiness comes from glutting ourselves with consumer goods. In this regard, the Genesis narrative is a telling critique of the way our society is geared.
Second, there is the desire to *see* and *know*. This desire is very much at home in contemporary society. Expressions like "Seeing is believing" give the impression that we could hardly survive without visual evidence. But common sense as well as Christian reflection both teach us that living also means knowing how to trust others, how to listen even if we do not understand everything.

The desire to *hear* only reinforces our inclination to be all-powerful. Here, too, Scripture helps to reverse this built-in tendency by showing that what really matters is listening to the Word of God — a word that urges us to hear the cry of the poor and underprivileged, a word summarized in the first Beatitude: *"Blessed are the poor."*

As Genesis 2 and 3 show, sin has given human beings a power of awesome destructiveness. But it is still a limited power; in Genesis, human beings are not the sole origin of evil. Adam and Eve come upon the serpent, one of God's creatures, who has already distorted God's prohibition. And so the Genesis narrative leaves room for a certain unknowing in the face of evil, an inability to fathom its depths. The narrative does not suppress its absurdity. But would evil be evil if it were no longer absurd?

CHAPTER 9

What Do We Mean by "Original Sin"?

1. Strictly speaking, the word *sin* means a voluntary *act* that sunders one's relationship with God. This is not an ideal word for describing the *state* into which all human beings are born. Moreover, the Greek Church tradition has preferred to stay away from the expression "original sin." In line with all of the most respected Catholic theologians, it needs to be said that the term *sin,* when used to describe the natural condition into which every child is born, is used only in a very *analogical* sense.

2. The term *original sin,* used to describe the native state into which we are born, needs to be distinguished from *originating sin,* the classic term for the sin of the first couple.

3. It is evident that original sin should not be thought of as some kind of stain or *genetic* flaw that is transmitted biologically, even if our unconscious desires would derive benefit from such a notion.

4. In the sinful acts we commit today, each of us recovers something of the experience described of Adam and Eve in Genesis. But our situation is unlike theirs in that we commit failings in a human setting where evil already has a strong grip on society because of the sins of all those who came before us.

5. Today many theologians (for example, Schoonenberg) use the term *original sin* to mean the thorough impossibility of a human being by birth to make a fundamental choice orienting his or her existence into conformity with God's design. This "structural" impossibility flows from the fact that a human being is never an isolated entity. By the very way we are structured or built, every one of us is dependent on the complex network of relationships into which we are immersed. This structuring network of persons is a network in which sin has already taken shape. This is the sin Saint John calls "the sin of the world" (John 1:29; 1 John 5:19).

So what the doctrine of original sin affirms is that, left to its own logic, with its whole backlog of sin, the world no longer has an in-grooved orientation toward the Creator and his call to love. That is why — the cross of Christ reminds us — this logic or trajectory of the world always tends to condemn the innocent, to reject the disfranchised, and at times even to use the Word of God as a means of dividing people by turning them away from the true God.

But let's not forget that Paul's claim that we are all linked together in a network of evil brings into view another, more radical claim — that we are all linked together in the network of salvation in Christ. Through Christ, the New Adam, and through the Spirit he gave us, it is possible for all human beings to reorient themselves toward the intended design of God, who alone humanizes. Paul's most basic conviction is that the power of Christ is stronger than the death-dealing power of sin: " ... *but where sin increased, grace abounded all the more ...* " (Romans 5:20); *"O death, where is thy victory?"* (1 Corinthians 15:55)

6. Is the idea of original sin contained in the concept of *collective sin* so frequently used today? I admit to lacking a totally clear view in the matter. But let me try to answer the question with a yes and a no.

Yes, to the extent that the expression *original sin* is meant to designate, among other things, a kind of structure that conditions human beings in society. In this sense, original sin is clearly a communal setting, a collective *state* of "sin" — that is, a rejection of God and therefore a state of human alienation. This state is constantly intensified by the sinful acts of individuals in a given community or society.

No, to the extent that the expression *original sin* means primarily a *state* we find ourselves in. If we want to avoid a blurred concept, which is always harmful, the expression *collective sin* should first of all mean an *act* of breaking off with God by a group at a precise given *moment* in its history. For example, collective sin would be the conscious refusal of a particular community, when an opportune moment presents itself, to take an active part in the struggle against some definite form of racism. In such a case, and in a certain way, we could say that collective sin is the reverse of the communion of saints. It is an expression of connivance or complicity on the part of each person in dividing a community. We see an example of this kind of sin in the worship of the golden calf by the people of Israel in chapter 32 of Exodus.

But it needs to be stressed clearly that sin, as an act, never exists without the making of a personal and responsible decision. Therefore, collective sin, in the strict sense of the term, always results in a pooling of individual sins — even if it cannot be reduced to their sum total — and takes a specific shape or form in the society.

So, it is out of the question to use the concept of collective sin to deny — or to excessively heighten — the personal responsibility of each person. To acknowledge the presence of collective sin always means also to try to pick out one's own personal responsibility in the sin.

So, in our catechesis and our penance services, let's try to keep matters straight by choosing one set of words when we are talking about *acts* for which we have direct personal and/or group responsibility, and different words when we are talking about collective *states* that these acts produce. If we do this, each person will be in a better position to judge his or her fidelity to God.

PART THREE

A CHRISTIAN UNDERSTANDING OF SIN

In this third part we will focus on several guidelines based on the Christian understanding of the reality we call sin. The Christian view of sin is an original one. To grasp what this means, we will look first at the origin or genesis of the sense of guilt. By doing that, we will see just how original the concept of sin is. We will also see that sin can be understood only in relation to God.

CHAPTER 10

Reflections on the Sense of Guilt

What is the sense of guilt? It is an *internal* reality within our psyche which gives us the feeling of being weighed down, the feeling of remorse, of standing before an inner tribunal that is ready to judge and inflict punishment. This is why the sense of guilt is accompanied by an inner demand for some act of reparation.

Psychologists, especially psychoanalysts, have a keen interest in the origins of the sense of guilt. Some of them focus on its very primal origins, linking it with the sensations of well-being and discomfort experienced by babies during their first months of life. Many other psychologists prefer not to speak of guilt being present until a child becomes conscious of failing to respond to the desire of the other, a desire which the child perceives as having the force of law. In this latter view, the sense of guilt is the experience of anguish over losing the esteem of a loved person who is seen as an aggressor. According to psychoanalyst Melanie Klein, who has done extensive research in this area, the first guilt feelings arise out of the infant's desire to devour its mother and its fear of reprisals.

Freud situated the origin of the guilt feeling at a rather late point in child development: the Oedipal stage. During this stage — between ages three and six — the child enters into a very complex set of loving and aggressive relationships with its parents. Through the presence and prohibitive word of its father, the child discovers that it must let go of the first object of its love, its mother. Along with other parental and cultural prohibitions, this fundamental prohibition of the father is interiorized, establishing a stance of watchfulness which Freud calls the superego. This stance functions in two ways: first of all as a tribunal ready to condemn, and as a reality which proposes an ideal to the child. According to Freud, then, guilt is fear in the presence of this superego which represses the desires experienced as forbidden by those who teach the child, or experienced as unworthy of the proposed ideal. The sense of guilt is thus a manifestation of anguish about being punished as well as fear of being abandoned by the one who is loved.

Following from this theory, there are several points worth noting.

First, Freud states that there can exist an *unconscious* sense of guilt. This is a curious expression; how can a sense be unconscious? What the subject is actually aware of is a "gnawing" in himself, a psychological uneasiness. The unconscious part is the guilt from which this uneasiness comes. In cases where this condition reaches the point of pathology, persons affected by this "gnawing" have been known to commit a deliberate unlawful act so that they can give a name to their dis-ease. Guilt, then, paradoxically becomes the cause of the unlawful act!

Second, the sense of guilt has a *social* dimension in that civilization uses the subject's aggressiveness against him in order to keep his violence within bounds acceptable to the human community. We can see this in our own lives; were it not for social pressure, the aggressiveness we turn against ourselves because of guilt feelings would be directed outward.

Third — and this is very important for our reflection on sin — the anguish of guilt *is not directly about the other* as the other really is. Rather, the anguish is the expression of a conflict that is primarily *within* the psyche. It could be said that guilt is a matter between me and myself. This is why psychologists as well as great spiritual guides have often emphasized that, at its core, guilt or remorse always has a self-centered dimension.

CHAPTER 11

Sin —
A Theological Concept

Guilt, as just described, is a purely psychic reality. In guilt feelings the others — my brother and my sister, or the Other who is God — are present only in an interiorized form. Guilt feelings do not take others into account as they are in real life.

The Christian understanding of guilt is just the opposite; it reverses this self-centered view. Revelation teaches that sin, far from being an "affair" between me and myself, is a reality which first of all concerns the *Other* who is God. The concept of sin, then, is clearly *theological.* Sin is a God-centered or, rather, a God-eccentric reality — because what it aims to do is to uncenter God. Let us see what this means.

Sin an Object of Revelation

The word *sin* points to a reality which involves our relationship with God. If God did not exist we could not speak of sin in its proper sense; there would be only failings against moral demands which mark the path to our becoming more human.

Sin must be understood from the outset as a blow to our relationship with God, as an act which creates an obstacle to receiving the gift of himself that God makes to our lives. That is why sin in its essence is ultimately *an object of revelation,* at least of revelation in a broad sense. So, if we know God fully only in the source and summit of revelation

— the Word made flesh — we know sin in its fullness only in perceiving the person of Jesus Christ.

Grasping the seriousness of sin and grasping the truth of the person of Christ take place in one single movement. So, when we speak of sin we are immediately in the presence of the Other, face-to-face with the radical otherness of God who is beyond all naming, who is jealous of any idol that could take his place.

Early on in the Old Testament the concept of sin was grasped through a central category which precisely conveys this otherness: the category of *covenant*. According to Scripture, to sin is to refuse to enter into the covenant of Yahweh, even though we realize that it brings happiness to humanity and glory to God. This otherness at the heart of the concept of sin is also expressed in the Old Testament by a host of images drawn from otherness experienced in human relationships, notably the experiences of fatherhood, motherhood, and the experience of the couple. Recall, for example, Isaiah 64:7-8, where sin is described as the ingratitude of a child toward its loving father. Recall Isaiah 49:15, where God is shown as expressing the love of a mother who could never forget the child of her womb. And recall chapter 2 in Hosea, where sin is presented as infidelity to a loving spouse. Already in the Old Testament the word *sin* means violence committed against a loving relationship between two beings who are vulnerable to each other.

This line of thought is picked up and developed in the New Testament, where God is finally identified as Love. Now it becomes evident that sin touches the Lord, the Spouse of the Church, touches the God who is Love. It is only within the light of love — a light that is possible only under the thrall of the Spirit — that the full import of sin is revealed in all its ramifications. Yet, curiously, our knowledge of sin is never total. Let us examine this last statement more closely.

Knowledge of Sin Never Total

One of the questions that is of greatest concern to Christians can be put this way: How can we know if we have sinned?

This question brings us up against one of the greatest paradoxes in the theology of sin. On the one hand, I cannot sin in the full sense of the word unless I freely and clearly intend to refuse relationship with God, unless I willingly and clearly put an idol in God's place. But at the same time, tradition has always affirmed that in every sinful act a person is marked by two great lacks in the area of knowledge. This, then, is the paradox: on the one hand I must *know* I am sinning in order to sin; on the other hand, knowledge about my sin is never total. Let us see if we can understand the two lacks of knowledge and the paradox they entail.

A partial lack of knowledge about
the consequences and gravity of my sin

Sin affects the Other by touching creation. It is logical, then, to say that only the Other can truly know how and to what extent he is affected. This means that the other who is my brother or sister and the Other who is God know something about my sin that I myself do not know.

Let us take an example. Suppose that in the conference room where I first presented these thoughts I had wanted to attack someone for not paying attention while I spoke; that I deliberately made a cutting remark, hoping it would hurt that person. In such a case, there would obviously be sin because I would have *deliberately* hurt that person. Now, it could have happened that this person was not paying attention even when I made the cutting remark, and was not affected by it. But it could just as easily have been that my remark fell upon very fragile psychological ground and brought to the surface childhood experiences of harsh reprimands which "broke" this person at a very young age. In this case my remark could have done considerable damage to the individual's personality — which, of course, I would have been unaware of. Therefore, the *objective* gravity of my sinful act would have partially escaped my knowledge. Only the person affected by my sin would know the extent of the harm I did.

But now, consider that the sin which touches my brother or sister also touches God. What this ultimately means is that only this God, "wounded" in his loving design, has a perfect knowledge of sin. This is why Saint Paul could say: "I am not aware of anything against myself, but I am not thereby acquitted. It is the Lord who judges me." (1 Corinthians 4:4)

Furthermore, we cannot grasp the actual extent of sin except through the *mediation of the Church* which is the bearer of God's Word, a word that is "living and active," that is "piercing" and "discerning the thoughts and intentions of the heart." (Hebrews 4:12) We will see later how revelation enables us to discover sin. For now let us focus on the important role played by the faith community — the Church — in this discovery. This role is operative, especially in the following areas which balance each other out:

— *The prophetic role.* We have a striking example of this role in the famous episode in 2 Samuel, chapter 12, where the prophet Nathan comes and tells David a parable that brings David's sin to the forefront of his consciousness. David had sinned gravely by murdering a man so that he, David, could commit adultery with the man's wife. Despite the grossness of his deed, David did not feel sinful. It took Nathan's prophetic intervention to make David realize the extent and objective gravity of his act.

This kind of challenging was a constant thing that prophets did in front of the people of Israel and their kings engulfed in sin. This is why, in today's society (which tends to confuse mercy and permissiveness), it is good to put emphasis on certain strong passages in the Old Testament. Take Ezekiel 3:17-18, for example, where God says to the prophet:

"*Son of man, I have made you a watchman for the house of Israel; . . . If I say to the wicked, 'You shall surely die,' and you give no warning, nor speak to warn the wicked from his wicked way, in order to save his life, that wicked man shall die in his iniquity, but his blood I will require at your hand.*"

By our Baptism all of us today are appointed "watchers" for the Christian and human communities. It is up to all of us to exercise a prophetic role and bear witness to the Word of God that calls and moves us to conversion. But lest it do more harm than good, this prophetic word must be rooted in deep humility. And above all, it must be *adapted* to actual situations; otherwise it crushes people with impossible demands instead of setting them free.

— *The role of fraternal correction.* This kind of correction is described explicitly in the New Testament; see Luke 17:3 (which says *"If your brother sins, rebuke him. . . "*) and Matthew 18:15-18. Because sin always affects the ecclesial body of Christ, the faith community has both the right and the duty to point out to its members how conduct it sees as sinful can affect people's attitude toward the kingdom. But here too, as with the prophetic word, great sensitivity is needed so that correction does not injure, or even destroy, persons. A certain number of people who have let go of their basic commitment would probably have been able to take hold of their lives before God if only they had found a brother or sister along the way to bring them to their senses and help them turn their lives around. Today we all need to question ourselves about the way we practice — or avoid practicing — fraternal correction.

A lack of knowledge about
the extent of my responsibility

To understand the reason behind this second lack of knowledge, it is important to see some of the many ways in which biblical anthropology relates to modern philosophical thought. The Bible distinguishes between a person's *heart* and its *acts.* The heart is the center of decisive choice (Matthew 22:37; 1 Corinthians 7:37); of encounter with God (Matthew 13:19); a hidden personal center which is of great importance because it is the source of good things and bad: "For out of the heart come evil thoughts, murder, adultery, fornication, theft, false witness, slander." (Matthew 15:19) The orientation of the heart is expressed in deeds. Yet, no individual act, nor the sum total of all its acts, totally expresses what is in the heart. So, even though heart and act are inseparable, they are distinct; neither can be reduced to the other.

In terms of modern philosophy, we could say that the heart is the center of a fundamental freedom that is capable of making a radical option for or against God, an option which engages the *whole person*. This radical option finds expression in the world only through particular acts which never totally exhaust a person's basic freedom. As the center of decision, this freedom of the human heart grounds, penetrates, and surpasses all particular acts.

In my view, this distinction between the heart and its acts helps us to understand the distinction that the New Testament makes between *sin* and *sins*. Saint John, for example, almost always speaks of sin in the singular — *hamartia*. He goes so far as to assert that "sin is lawlessness" (1 John 3:4) — that is, the proud rejection of God who saves.

As for Saint Paul, he, like his contemporaries, makes use of lists of sins (see, for example, 1 Corinthians 6:9-11). But Paul makes it clear that sins such as these are all the result of sin in the sense of a deliberate refusal to acknowledge God, the Creator whom every human being is in principle capable of recognizing (Romans 1:18-31 and 5:12-17). Paul attributes such importance to this use of the word *sin* that he presents it as a kind of personified power.

When a person's heart is molded by this power of sin — in other words, when a person's radical option is turned away from God — the Christian tradition then speaks of "*mortal sin.*" This is the one reality that truly deserves the name *sin;* the term is used only analogously when we speak of "venial sin." According to the better theologians, venial sin means an imperfect obedience to the will of God or a halt on our journey toward God rather than a rupture in our relationship with our Creator and Savior.

In view of the fact that many Christians today are profoundly ill at ease with the expression *mortal sin,* let us digress a bit to focus on it. With persons who have the ability to understand and appreciate it without excessive anxiety, it may be good to draw the distinction between mortal and venial sin for the following two reasons:

The first reason is drawn from tradition. The expressions *mortal sin* and *venial sin* are not found as such in Scripture. But we do find there a clear distinction between two kinds of sin. According to Paul, for example, there are faults which exclude one from the kingdom of God (see Galatians 5:19-21 and 1 Corinthians 6:9-10). And Saint John says that the refusal to love causes a person to abide in death (1 John 3:14-15). Jesus, furthermore, speaks of logs or beams in the eyes of those who pass judgment on one another. And, speaking of pardon for sins, Jesus also enjoins us to pray for it daily in the Our Father (Matthew 6:12 and Luke 11:4). It cannot be that these "trespasses" are all of equal gravity.

As for the liturgical, patristic, and theological tradition, the teaching found there is explicit: contrary to certain doctrinal deviations, the tradition has always maintained that not all sins result in the death of one's relationship with God. Therefore, some sins are less serious than others. They are, in other words, venial sins.

A theological reason for the distinction would be as follows: sin makes the power of death felt in real life. As we have already noted, the death of a person's relationship with God always translates into the breakdown of human relationships.

Underneath everything, our reluctance to use the term *mortal* could be an indication that we are victims of a social mind-set that tries to keep death under wraps. This possibility at least deserves some thought.

Having digressed on the topic of mortal sin, let us return to the question of knowledge about the extent of my responsibility. This knowledge, I said, is always marked by a lack of knowledge. The only things accessible to my knowledge are my outward acts, and these are an expression of freedom which is deeply conditioned psychologically, physiologically, and socially. That being so, it is impossible to know with *absolute* certainty whether my heart is in a situation of openness to, or radical rejection of, the kingdom of God. This is because, ultimately, I am unable to draw an unmistakable dividing line between what is due to conditioning and what is a product of my freedom.

In stating this, I am simply maintaining continuity with the classic traditional doctrine formulated by Saint Thomas Aquinas: "And hence man cannot judge with certainty that he has grace, according to 1 Cor. iv. 3,4: *'But neither do I judge my own self . . . but He that judgeth me is the Lord.'* " (*Summa Theologica,* Ia, IIae, 112, 5) This teaching was reaffirmed by the Council of Trent, which stated: " . . . no one can know with the certainty of faith, which cannot be subject to error, that he has obtained the grace of God." (Decree on Justification, chapter IX, 1534) Spiritual giant that she was, Saint Joan of Arc had grasped this truth, and would say to her accusers: "You ask whether I am in the state of grace? If I am, may God keep me there. If I am not, may God put me there!"

In order to judge the seriousness of sin, we must try to *interpret* our particular acts. In this way they can be taken as *signs* of the condition of our hearts. Saint Thomas had no hesitation in using the phrase "know conjecturally" to qualify knowledge of sin. Having used that phrase, he goes on to say: " . . . and thus anyone may know he has grace, when he is conscious of delighting in God. . . . " (Ia, IIae, 112, 5)

In everyday circumstances, then, how are we to judge the seriousness of our sin? Aside from what I will say later about signs of the presence of sin, I think the following guidelines can be offered:

If the sinful acts that I have done are objectively grave and if I seem to have done them with great freedom of choice, it is then probable that my heart is far from God or — as the catechism would put it — no longer in the state of grace. In that case I have the moral certainty that I have sinned seriously or "mortally." I have the moral certainty that I have desired and brought about the death of my relationship with God. On the other hand, take the case of Christians who sense that what spiritual writers call "the fine point of their will" is rooted in God — Christians who sense that in its basic option their life as a whole is in harmony with the Gospel. Such Christians would have a solid reason for asking themselves whether frequent "falls," in some particular area of life in which these persons are clearly weak, are really serious rejections of God's love. In such a case a person may at times have moral certainty that his or her failings flow from weakness and not from deliberate and free choice at its deepest level. In the case of a person whose fundamental option is good, mortal sin is not all that frequent because of God's enlivening love at work in the person. This is why I think that mortal sin in the life of a Christian who prays, who is united to the Church, and who tries to love is probably quite rare. Nevertheless, let me make two points:

1. This first point consists of a passage from *Persona humana,* the 1976 Vatican "Declaration on Certain Questions Concerning Sexual Ethics." This document rightly recalls the following:

"In reality, it is precisely the fundamental option which in the last resort defines a person's moral disposition. But it can be *completely changed by particular acts,* especially when, as often happens, these have been prepared for by previous more superficial acts. Whatever the case, it is wrong to say that particular acts are not enough to constitute mortal sin. . . . A person therefore sins mortally not only when his action comes from direct contempt for love of God and neighbor, but also when he consciously and freely, for whatever reason, chooses something which is seriously disordered." (10) What this passage points out is that there are in our lives clearly identifiable acts which make such a difference that they can radically involve the fundamental option and be signs that it has undergone change.

2. My second remark is meant to emphasize that neither a profound break in relationship with God nor close intimacy with God is ever irreversible.

In this regard, it is good to recall the words of the Old Testament: "But when a righteous man turns away from his righteousness and commits iniquity . . . none of the righteous deeds which he has done shall be remembered. . . . " (Ezekiel 18:24) And conversely, "if a wicked man turns away from all his sins . . . he shall surely live; he shall not die."

In conclusion, we can see how misplaced the twofold lack of knowledge renders any attempt to get to the bottom of human responsibility for sin. From time to time an exploration of that kind may help a person to sort out the inner workings that lead up to his failings. It can help a person to get a grip on his life by himself or with help from others. But more often this kind of probing betrays a streak of self-centeredness that takes the form of wallowing in misery and humiliation, or that tries to justify oneself before God. It makes one wonder: What must a person with such an attitude think God is like? It would have to be God as seen through the eyes of Cain or God viewed as a courtroom judge establishing guilt in order to throw the book at the accused!

On those occasions in the Gospels when Jesus met people and forgave them, he showed little interest in drawn-out recitals of sin. Look, for example, at the passage where Jesus pardons a paralytic (Matthew 9:1-8; Mark 2:1-12; and Luke 5:17-26) or the time he pardons the adulterous woman (John 8:3-11) or the word of Christ to the sinful woman who anoints his feet with perfume (Luke 7:36-50). In these encounters, what matters to Jesus is not the details but the sinner's heart discovering him as He who loves, as He whose love can set us free.

CHAPTER 12

First Sign of Sin: Transgression

To conclude this brief reflection on sin, I would like to examine some of the means available to Christians for telling in a general way when an act needs God's forgiveness — in other words, when sin is involved. We will look at five criteria that can be considered signs of a breach with God. No one of these signs is clear-cut; each is marked by a radical ambiguity. So we need to be clear about how these signs do and do not point to sin. The first sign we will examine is transgression.

By the word *transgression* I mean a going beyond the bounds of a prohibition — a moral rule or a social law. The connection between sin and transgression is not always easy to establish, but we can summarize it in this general formula: every sin is a transgression but not every transgression is a sin.

Every sin is a transgression. Sin, as we saw, is a transgression against the fundamental law of life given by God. However, not all transgressions are sins. Why? For the following reasons:

— First of all, it is possible for a person to go against a prohibition *involuntarily*. A person can, as they say, "get carried away." Flying off the handle at a neighbor, for example, can be more a sign of weakness than a sin.

— It is also possible for a person to be *ignorant* about the fact that an ethical prohibition even exists in some area of life. Or a person may not see how the breaking of a particular moral or social law affects his relationship with God. Here we are in the area of what moral theologians have called "invincible ignorance." For example, we can understand how a young person raised in a Nazi environment might think that persecuting Jews is a good thing to do. Objectively, persecuting Jews is a truly serious evil. But to the extent that this person's social conditioning makes him blind to the fact that he is perpetrating evil, he does not sin in God's eyes.

Another example: today many people cheat on income taxes, cheat on exams, or pad expense accounts, with the idea that "This is how the game is played." To the extent that these people are honestly not conscious of any wrongdoing, the transgressions are objectively evil but not subjectively sinful.

The theological tenet that we must follow our conscience, even if it is based on a false understanding, is not only not a sin but a duty. This doctrine, however, is no justification for "anything goes," because it also points out that we can be responsible through lack of effort for a mistaken or uninformed conscience. We must be prepared at all times to develop a more enlightened conscience by listening to the Word of God from the Christian faith community and from our other brothers and sisters.

— It is also possible that a particular prohibition can be *dehumanizing*. In that case, it is the transgression that becomes a sign of obedience to God and a sign of love. An example would be Jesus' transgression of overly strict prohibitions concerning work on the sabbath. As Jesus pointed out, "The sabbath was made for man, not man for the sabbath. . . . " (Mark 2:27) Thus, it is possible for transgressions of overly strict or misguided human regulations to be real signs of love. The example of Jesus is an invitation to probe the foundations of the human ethical norms we receive.

Whenever there is question of transgressing a Church prohibition, a person must be especially attentive to exercising Christian responsibility, one's true freedom as a son or daughter of God. This freedom should never be an excuse for permissiveness; it should be a taking of responsibility in the Spirit for a decision made in the face of conflicting values. The criteria for judging one's responsibility in such a situation can be, among others, the following: a true spirit of prayer; serious reflection; a taking care to have one's genuineness probed by a member of the Church — a priest, a friend, or even one's community; and a humility so searching that it could lead one to recognize that he or she is making a mistake.

— It can happen, finally, that it becomes necessary to transgress one prohibition in order to safeguard a more basic prohibition.

There are many instances of this in one's moral life. To give an example, the taking of another person's life is always a very serious matter. But it is possible that this act may be justified if one's own life or the lives of loved ones have been put in serious jeopardy by unjust aggression from the person in question. This is not an uncommon experience for individuals who live in urban centers. The same basic point arises in states where the law permits capital punishment. The point also comes to the fore when a nation contemplates going to war against an unjust aggressor nation. The position that self-defense is justified rests on the conviction that the prohibition against killing another person yields to a more basic right — the right of an individual or a community to hold their own lives or fundamental values in freedom.

Transgression, then, is an especially ambiguous indication of sin. This is so mainly because of the desire for total power we all possess from infancy. This tendency often causes within us a truly harmful confusion: *the confusion between weakness and sin.*

By weakness I mean an *involuntary* transgression against an order established by a social code or by ethical demands. An example would be a damaging remark that slips out in a heated moment — the kind of statement a person immediately regrets.

A transgression — for example, shoving someone in a fit of

anger — can be the result of two possibilities. It can be the result of a very free decision on my part. In that case it can be called *sin*. Or, on the other hand, it can be the result of personal limitations which prevent me from being in total control of myself. Some of the things I do escape the control of my will; they "get the upper hand." When that is the case the transgression should not be called sin, but *weakness*.

To help clarify what I mean, look at the diagram that you see here.

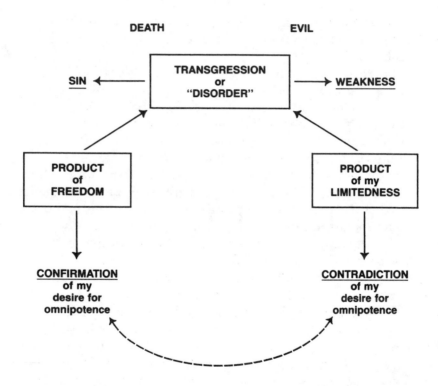

This distinction would present no problem if the human person were not possessed of the *desire to be all-powerful* which, in the Adam and Eve story, shows up in the form of a desire for the forbidden fruit.

How does this desire for ultimate power affect our willingness or refusal to recognize ourselves as sinners? It can take two possible forms, both of which sometimes operate in the same person at more or less the same time.

The first possibility consists of calling something a sin when it is only a result of weakness. Certain people find it very difficult to admit that they are not in absolute control of themselves. "After all these years of trying to be calm with my husband," a person told me, "I keep falling back into my same old rut of anger. I'm a sinner, that's all there is to it." When I led this person to reflect on the pattern of her behavior, she realized that freedom had very little to do with it — that her outbursts of anger were much more the result of personal limitations than deliberate sin. She told me: "If I understand correctly, what you're doing is getting me to realize that I'm not really sinning. You're taking everything away from me!"

That's right. This person suddenly realized that deep down she liked calling herself a sinner. What she was doing was reinforcing her desire to be all-powerful.

There is also a reverse strategy. There are people who sin quite deliberately, but the choice they make leaves them disturbed and humiliated; they have a wounded ego due to the fact that they have tarnished the shining image they had of themselves. As a result, they try to escape their discomfort by claiming that they did what they did out of weakness, not sin.

We need to be aware of this double strategy. It lurks in all of us to some extent, and it works in different ways in different areas of life. In some people the first strategy is at work in the area of sex; some people would rather call themselves sinners than admit they have a sexual problem to cope with. On the other hand, the second strategy is at work in these same people when it comes to professional ethics. They use rationalizations like "It's a jungle out there" and "Let's be realistic" to cover up dishonesty and injustice.

As we noted earlier in regard to psychoanalysis, it is never a simple matter to determine the exact extent of one's responsibility. It is possible, however, to sort out whether it is my personal limitation or a perversion of my freedom that has the upper hand.

Lastly, I would like to point out that our little diagram on page 64 can help us to understand the limitations of certain views. Some people say that sinful humanity is the origin of all the world's evils, including biological death. They maintain that without sin there would be no suffering or death. One problem with making humanity the exclusive source of all the world's evils is that this endows humankind with a destructive power of unbelievable magnitude — a grand reinforcement of the desire to be all-powerful! Views of that kind are tantamount to a denial of human limitation. It would seem more realistic to say that we human beings are just as limited in our power for evil as we are in our power for good. Since the evidence does not support any claim that we are the God of goodness, there are those who sometimes prefer to think of themselves as the god of evil — the devil. Chapters 2 and 3 of Genesis are a help in this regard. By teaching that we are definitely neither God nor the devil, the Adam and Eve narrative can help us to avoid denying our limitations.

CHAPTER 13

Second Sign of Sin: Deviation

By the word *deviation* I mean a state of nonconformity to a classic norm received within a human group.

Besides other results, being deviant can produce two types of reaction in a person: having a pseudosense of sin and being a pseudoprophet.

— In the case of a pseudosense of sin, the interiorizing of social norms can cause a person to believe, at first, that his or her deviation is immoral and sinful. Rather than calmly accept the fact of being different, some people tend to consider themselves guilty and go on from there to draw attention and sympathy from others. Due to social pressure, there are people today who would rather see themselves as sinners than nonconformists.

— Deviance can go so far as to be pseudoprophetic. This happens when deviants decide that society is the real deviant and that their own behavior, not that of the majority, should be considered normative.

The relation between deviation and sin is not easy to spell out. Deviation can be an expression of a desire to cut oneself off from God by a deliberate refusal to follow social and ecclesial norms which foster human growth and freedom. But it can also express basic Gospel values — for example, a life of nonviolence. In cases of this latter kind the deviation may express a truly prophetic challenge.

It is also possible for a person to decide, with mature deliberation, that deviation is a duty. The person may believe that this is the only way he or she can avoid a predicament brought on by, say, past failings or psychological problems. A deviant situation such as that of a person who is divorced and remarried certainly cannot be considered normative. But it is possible that the person in that situation is not in a subjective state of sin.

People who live in such situations need a deep willingness to stay in dialogue with the faith community in order to safeguard their relationship with God. In turn, the community needs to remain open to dialogue, refusing to make hasty judgments or to ostracize — acts that do violence to the Gospel.

CHAPTER 14

Third Sign of Sin: Suffering

People often try to pin responsibility for their suffering on someone else; none of us is very good at bearing up under the absurdity of evil. Often, too, a person will blame himself for his suffering, believing that he is getting what he deserves for his sins. You see this kind of reaction in the well-known Gospel passage about the man born blind — John 9:1-3. When the disciples ask Jesus whether the man's blindness is due to his own sin or to that of his parents, Jesus rejects the pat equation: suffering = consequences of actual sin. He answers that neither the blind man nor his parents have sinned.

Still, there are other biblical passages which promise joy, peace, and happiness to those who follow Jesus and live by Gospel precepts. And unhappiness is promised to money-grubbers, exploiters of others, and false prophets (Luke 6:24-26). Along the same line, many passages in Scripture link sin with the powers of evil and with sickness. How are we to understand all this?

Let us recall what we said earlier. Sin is the rejection of what makes us truly human; God's plan for human creatures is that they grow to their full stature as adult human beings — whole, free adoptive sons and daughters. In terms of this process, sin is always a dehumanizing element. It causes us to regress; it stunts integral human development. It is therefore inevitable that sin produce situations in which people experience the painful consequences of their alienation.

To avoid pitfalls, however, we do well to distinguish between what theologians call *physically endured evil* (for example, blindness) and *moral evil* (sin). It is in our nature as creatures to undergo failure and suffering, to see our "best laid plans" go awry, and to live in the shadow of death. These types of suffering — the physical experience of evil — are certainly not immediate consequences of sin; they are simply the consequences of our human condition.

On the other hand, the consequences of sin arise partly from reacting badly to physical evils. Sufferings such as blindness, for example, can become occasions for bitterness toward God or even loss of faith, instead of being occasions for deepened faith and humility.

Evils also arise from the way people exploit or manipulate one another. This is the stuff from which sin creates its "body" in the world — stabilized patterns of evil which influence people's lives. Gustave Martelet put it very well when he wrote: "It is evil becoming an organic presence within individuals and within the world. It is the spiritual misery of humanity, in the form of structures we have fashioned or acquired, taking control of us even though it is a product of our own freedom." The *Handbook for Today's Catholic* describes the same reality when it says: "Patterns of evil can be institutionalized. Injustice, for example, can become part of a group's way of life, embedded in laws and social customs. Such patterns, in a ripple effect, contaminate the attitudes and actions of people in that environment. The influence of these patterns can be so subtle that people enmeshed in them may literally be unaware of the evil they promote."

This organized tearing-down of the fabric of life exacts its toll in human suffering. And on top of that, another problem arises from the fact that some people mistakenly blame this body of sin in the world on "life" or "Mother Nature," when what it is in reality is sin embodied in the world. It is, for example, a mistake to call Black Lung — a condition that has destroyed the health and lives of generations of American coal miners in Appalachia — a mere "occupational hazard." Another example would be to see no connection between the problem of alcoholism and its aggravation by slick television and magazine ads from breweries and distilleries corrupted by the desire for profits. Here, and elsewhere, there is an ongoing tendency to confuse the two levels of evil: the physical evil we experience as a result of our human limitations — and moral evil or sin, a result of our human freedom.

Suffering, then, is another sign that is quite ambiguous when it comes to telling whether sin is present. At times, suffering can show that a given group or person has indeed sinned. But it is also an invitation for each of us to recognize the limitations of our human condition.

There are genuine prophets who bring God's plans for us into focus and proclaim them in season and out, helping us to sort out suffering as a symptom of sin from suffering as a reminder of our human finitude — our "being-for-death," as Heidegger called it.

CHAPTER 15

Fourth Sign of Sin: Objective Content of the Act

It is accurate to say that the objective seriousness of behavior can be an especially pertinent sign that gravely sinful matter is objectively present. Indeed, if an individual's conduct is very destructive to self and others and if the person engages in that conduct with full possession of his or her freedom, it is probable that the person sins gravely.

Nevertheless, a problem can arise in regard to a person's awareness of the objective seriousness of his or her behavior. A person's grasp of the meaning of such behavior can often fall prey to unconscious "strategies" or be seriously affected by the pressure of social conditioning.

This is all the more true regarding sinful matter in the areas of sexuality and aggression. We are all acquainted with the assertion that in matters of chastity all sins are objectively mortal, a view that has been maintained for centuries in Church tradition. Theologians are constantly seeking to refine our understanding of this teaching, asking questions such as: Are we speaking of the same gravely disordered act when we speak of masturbation by an infant, by an adolescent, and by an adult? Greater clarity is sometimes gained by such questioning. Over the course of decades, for example, theologians scarcely disputed the belief that colonial exploitation by one nation over another was not gravely sinful matter. Today, now that such questioning goes on, we are in a better position to see that insisting on sexual gravity while neglecting a massive issue such as colonial aggression could be a case of what Jesus meant by "straining out the gnat and swallowing a camel." (Matthew 23:24)

We can see, then, that if the matter of sin provides a good indication of its seriousness, a critical examination first needs to be made of the thinking that weighs how serious the matter is. This critical examination should always be made in the back-and-forth of dialogue with the more reliable discoveries of the behavioral sciences, the best findings of biblical exegesis, and the solid guidelines of tradition.

Having said that, we may ask whether it is appropriate today to want updated lists of serious sins. There are people who shake their heads and smile at traditional lists such as the sins against the theological virtues and the seven capital sins. These people have a point; the old lists portrayed sin as almost a thing existing on its own, and they avoided analyzing what goes on in the real world.

Still, a theological vision that has lasted for a long time in Church tradition can never be set aside lightly. The persistence of these lists through the centuries may well be a sign that they tapped into some basic human and theological truths. For just that reason, I did a study of these traditional sin lists. What I found is that, on the whole, these lists are packed with relevance. There is no question about it where sins against the theological virtues are concerned — that is how seriously Scripture takes these sins.

To sin against *faith* is perhaps the deepest source of all other sins because ultimately such a sin is a refusal to believe in the one God who is Creator and Savior. It leads almost inevitably to idolatry. The whole of Scripture demonstrates that sin is always a form of idolatry.

To sin against *hope* is to refuse to believe that a future is possible for the world, for others, or for oneself. It is to refuse to believe that the power of God is able to make its presence felt in weakness and to confound the "wisdom" of the world (1 Corinthians, chapter 1).

To sin against *charity* is to turn in on oneself in an excessive, self-serving way instead of opening one's heart to others who are in need. It is to show that one has not yet welcomed the One who is Love and who wants human beings to have life.

"All well and good," some will say. "The sins against the theological virtues still have a lot to them. But what about the capital sins? What can these old labels possibly mean to us today? Absolutely nothing!"

Is it really that certain? If we take a close look at the human underpinnings of these sin lists, we might just discover something pertinent to our lives. Let's examine each of the capital sins in terms of what is actually happening in the human race.

The main form of human alienation dividing people today, it seems to me, is the cherished desire we all have for total control. Recall what we said about our egg diagram in chapter 5. Our "cult" of this desire for omnipotence brings us right back to the sin of *pride,* which Church tradition has always denounced as the number one capital sin.

Another contemporary form of sin can be found in the deliberate refusal to accept differences; in the desire to possess what the other person possesses. This, it seems to me, brings us right back to the capital sin known as *envy.*

Sin often takes shape in us by a wrong use of our aggressiveness. Contemporary ethical reflection shows that what human moral effort needs first is to undergo a harnessing of violence — that most of the world's evils are rooted in a passive or active acquiescence in mutual, murderous violence. Following this line of thought, we are right back with the capital sin of *anger,* which is a wrong way to channel aggressiveness.

Our whole society is based on the pursuit of profits, often at the expense of persons. The human work force is used to make the rich richer and the poor poorer. So, a wrong attitude toward money is one of the most pregnant forms of sin in our society. In tradition, this wrong approach to money was called *avarice* or *greed.*

We live in a consumer society that acts as if we cannot be saved or attain happiness except by glutting our desires. In the words of one critical observer, "It is the great grub society organized around the business of eating." Church tradition had suspected that the pursuit of oral pleasure was something to be concerned about and denounced it as the capital sin of *gluttony*.

Another form of sin revolves around the exploiting of the difference between the sexes, around man's subjugation of woman, around a wrong attitude toward the body's sexuality. Tradition called it *lust*.

Lastly, there is a sin that we see more and more today. It is the sin of giving in to spiritual apathy due to the difficulties of living the faith in today's world, due to the crisis in which fidelity to God is being put to the test by a rampant godlessness — a spiritual stagnation that prevents Christians from plunging into the struggle for God. Tradition described this seventh capital sin by the term *sloth*.

And so we see a consistent pattern running through the story of how human beings say no to God. The best of Christian reflection has always known how to pick out the weak spots in human nature, the points where sin finds its openings. From a pedagogical viewpoint, it might be best not to call these weak points "capital sins." But from the updated lists we just went through, it seems to me that they give us some firm guidelines for examining our consciences today.

CHAPTER 16

Fifth Sign of Sin: The Feeling of Guilt

One of the signs that Christians frequently use to tell whether sin is present in their lives is the sense of remorse or guilt feelings. Many people tell themselves, "I don't feel any remorse; that's a sign I haven't done anything wrong." Or they will say the opposite: "I feel a lot of remorse; I must have sinned pretty seriously." That kind of thinking is simply too simple.

We need to be clear about the connection between sin and guilt feelings. Quite frequently, the feeling of guilt is all out of proportion to the seriousness of the act. In some cases strong guilt feelings follow in the wake of acts that objectively are not very serious, and in other cases there is practically no sense of guilt after acts that are objectively very serious indeed. We already saw why this happens: the feeling of guilt is something that takes place between me and myself, whereas sin is a reality that affects my relationship with the Other who is God. This means that we need to guard against two attitudes into which we can drift at various times in life, each of them as misguided as the other. Here they are in brief outline:

First attitude: refusal to admit we are sinners; denial of sin

This was the attitude of David after he arranged the death of one of his soldiers, Uriah the Hittite, and slept with

Uriah's wife, Bathsheba. David refused to recognize that he had sinned. This example shows, as Paul Ricoeur has pointed out, how guilt is often a self-centered self-deception.

Look, for example, at the words some people use when they arrive late for a meeting: "*I'm* sorry *I'm* late, *but....*" You can see through the words to their self-centered pattern: *I* excuse *myself* — and the deception: *but....* A true sense of guilt would be expressed more like this: "Please excuse me; I'm late."

Jesus had strong words about evading guilt when he said: "*... the light has come into the world, and men loved darkness rather than light, because their deeds were evil. For every one who does evil hates the light, and does not come to the light, lest his deeds should be exposed.*" (John 3:19-20)

To some degree we all try to deny guilt in certain areas of our lives. But revelation has a way of exposing the self-centeredness of our spontaneous (or sometimes deliberate) attempts to evade guilt. It does so notably by revealing the deep seriousness of sin, a seriousness that comes to light in a number of ways:

— *We have a basic inability to get out of sin by our own efforts.* We can try to overlook or to gloss over our radical helplessness, but revelation insists on the fact that we are "bound" by the sin that has become embodied in us. This is how Saint Paul describes the person under the control of sin: "...I do not do what I want, but I do the very thing I hate.... I can will what is right, but I cannot do it. For I do not do the good I want, but the evil I do not want is what I do." (Romans 7:15,18-19) We are so enslaved to sin that only God our Savior, only Jesus Christ the Messiah, can empower us to turn back to our Creator.

— Sin has *irremediable consequences* which even God cannot take away. Religion teachers have been known to commit the classic error of presenting God's forgiveness as a reinstatement of lost integrity. In real life, due to his self-limitation in relation to creation, God cannot prevent acts, once they are done, from having consequences — sometimes decisive ones. What God can do is make possible a new future for the sinner in spite of the harm done to self, others, and society.

— Sin is serious because it *affects God*. This is one of the central revelations of Scripture. Our sin is not only an injury at the human level; in some way it also affects God, a point brought out in the International Theological Commission Report for the 1983 World Synod of Bishops.

In keeping with a traditional line of thought, there are contemporary theologians who say that sin causes a kind of suffering in God. Conscious of the fact that they are using language analogically, these theologians say that sin harms God by affecting his plan, whose glory is "the human person fully alive" in his presence.

When I am tempted to evade the fact that I have sinned, tempted to evade my real responsibility, a look at the cross of Christ and an attentive listening to the Word of God have a way of reminding me that sin is always a dealer of death to humanity and a dealer of suffering to God.

Nevertheless, I would point out that even this insight can manage to feed our desire to be all-powerful. What power there can be in the discovery that we can actually make God suffer! This is why the traditional theme of God's suffering needs to be seen within the framework of the biblical theme of divine immutability (see, for example, Psalm 102:24-28; Jeremiah 7:9; Malachi 3:6; James 1:17). By recalling to us that God is never destroyed by sin, this theme helps shatter the ever-recurring illusion that our power can equal that of God.

Second attitude: exaggeration of guilt

In the final analysis this attitude is one of self-contempt. It consists in cultivating guilt to the point of belittling oneself and wallowing in false humility. Atheist philosophers as well as spiritual ones have always emphasized that this kind of self-disparagement is very narcissistic. As Nietzche put it, "Whoever despises himself delights in despising himself." Spiritual guides have advised us to be gentle in correcting ourselves because they see excessive anger at self as a manifestation of excessive self-seeking.

Here too, regarding the wrong use of guilt, revelation puts things into proper perspective.

— First, revelation reminds me that God's love for me depends in no way on humiliations I heap on myself. God does not love people for putting themselves down. God wants us to be humble, but in the sense of calmly accepting ourselves as we are. And what God loves even more is to see us standing tall as responsible sons and daughters.

— Second, when revelation unmasks my sin, it also reveals God's offer of forgiveness. Scripture always links the two proclamations of sin and salvation. This is why, as Paul Ricoeur puts it so well, Christians do not believe in sin, they believe in the "remission of sin." So, if we keep our eyes focused on the God of Scripture, we cannot possibly wrap ourselves up in degrading guilt. God's forgiveness is always there, ready with a new offer of welcome to himself and to others, even though I may feel like closing myself off in remorse.

— Finally, revelation tells me that I do not have to "pay" for my past failures. The mind sometimes derives unhealthy "kickbacks" from wanting to do expiation in the sense of paying a price for past failures. The whole of Scripture tells me that God does not ask for that kind of expiation. All that God asks is that we live in harmony with the forgiveness we receive from him. God wants us to receive his forgiveness as a gift that we develop, a talent that creates a deep joy within us.

And so it is that our reflections on sin end up in a reflection on God's forgiveness. It is not by mere chance that we end this way, because forgiveness is the highest and most perfect gift we could imagine. To be Christian and to admit being a sinner means to discover that this perfect gift is offered to me right at the heart of my weakest and least admirable self. *"There is therefore now no condemnation for those who are in Christ Jesus. For the law of the Spirit of life in Christ Jesus has set me free from the law of sin and death."* (Romans 8:1-2)

ABOUT THE AUTHOR

Father Xavier Thévenot, a Salesian of Don Bosco, teaches moral theology at the Catholic Institute of Paris. Firmly rooted in Church tradition, Father Thévenot's theological work is carefully attuned to the behavioral and social sciences. This book is based on talks given at the Jean-Bart Center in Paris during the academic year 1980-1981.